Published by Spark Publications in 2016
First edition; First printing

Design and writing © 2016 Bonni Goldberg
Cover design by Jessica Martin

All rights reserved. No part of this book may be reproduced or transmitted in any form or by any means, including but not limited to information storage and retrieval systems, electronic, mechanical, photocopy, recording, etc. without written permission from the copyright holder.

ISBN 978-0-9967524-1-1

More than the Jewish People have kept the Sabbath, the Sabbath has kept the Jews.

Ahad Ha'am

Welcome to **your** Family Shabbat Journal.

Shabbat is our weekly Jewish holiday. Officially, it begins at sundown on Friday and ends Saturday night when three stars appear in the sky or approximately 25 hours after it began on Friday night.

Around the world, and around your community, Jews celebrate Shabbat with a spectrum of customs and rituals. The most common thread in these celebrations is that they're family centered. Whether your family observes a traditional version of Shabbat or Friday night is pizza delivery and a family movie, the foundation of Shabbat is coming together every week to set apart time from daily work for rest, appreciation, and gratitude.

Judaism values the power of words. A journal is the perfect place to collect words of reflection, memories, and intentions. *Our Family Shabbat Journal* is for your family to create and record how Shabbat expresses your family and to enhance everyone's experience. For the young and the creative, the journal includes weekly space for visual expression: draw, collage, or add stickers.

There are numerous ways to use the weekly pages. Experiment:

- Ask everyone to contribute to each prompt
- Ask whoever feels inspired by a given prompt to contribute
- Assign a single family member to a specific prompt
- Take turns each week with one family member or group of family members responding to all the prompts
- Any other options your family thinks up

If your Shabbat observance includes refraining from writing or drawing, use this journal as part of preparing for Shabbat (the first page) and then as part of marking its end (the second page).

Shabbat Shalom!

Date _____

**This week,
I'm grateful for:**

_____
_____
_____
_____
_____

**One thing
I learned this week:**

_____
_____
_____
_____
_____

**I helped someone
this week by:**

_____
_____
_____
_____
_____

**The best thing to
happen this week:**

_____
_____
_____
_____
_____

This week's family blessing:

Our Shabbat this week:
(foods, activities, family, friends, events, pets, etc.)

_____
_____
_____
_____
_____
_____
_____
_____

Draw, doodle, stick...

Date _____

This week,
I'm grateful for:

_____
_____
_____
_____
_____

One thing
I learned this week:

_____
_____
_____
_____
_____

I helped someone
this week by:

_____
_____
_____
_____
_____

The best thing to
happen this week:

_____
_____
_____
_____
_____

This week's family blessing:

Our Shabbat this week:
(foods, activities, family, friends, events, pets, etc.)

_____
_____
_____
_____
_____
_____
_____
_____

Draw, doodle, stick...

Date _____

**This week,
I'm grateful for:**

_____
_____
_____
_____
_____

**One thing
I learned this week:**

_____
_____
_____
_____
_____

**I helped someone
this week by:**

_____
_____
_____
_____
_____

**The best thing to
happen this week:**

_____
_____
_____
_____
_____

This week's family blessing:

Our Shabbat this week:
(foods, activities, family, friends, events, pets, etc.)

_____
_____
_____
_____
_____
_____
_____
_____
_____

Draw, doodle, stick...

Date _____

**This week,
I'm grateful for:**

_____
_____
_____
_____
_____

**One thing
I learned this week:**

_____
_____
_____
_____
_____

**I helped someone
this week by:**

_____
_____
_____
_____
_____

**The best thing to
happen this week:**

_____
_____
_____
_____
_____

This week's family blessing:

Our Shabbat this week:
(foods, activities, family, friends, events, pets, etc.)

_____
_____
_____
_____
_____
_____
_____
_____

Draw, doodle, stick...

Date _____

This week,
I'm grateful for:
_____
_____
_____
_____
_____
_____

One thing
I learned this week:
_____
_____
_____
_____
_____
_____

I helped someone
this week by:
_____
_____
_____
_____
_____

The best thing to
happen this week:
_____
_____
_____
_____
_____

This week's family blessing:

Our Shabbat this week:
(foods, activities, family, friends, events, pets, etc.)

_____
_____
_____
_____
_____
_____
_____
_____
_____

Draw, doodle, stick...

Date _____

This week,
I'm grateful for:
_____
_____
_____
_____
_____

One thing
I learned this week:
_____
_____
_____
_____
_____

I helped someone
this week by:
_____
_____
_____
_____
_____

The best thing to
happen this week:
_____
_____
_____
_____
_____

This week's family blessing:

Our Shabbat this week:
(foods, activities, family, friends, events, pets, etc.)

_____
_____
_____
_____
_____
_____
_____
_____

Draw, doodle, stick...

Date _____

**This week,
I'm grateful for:**

_____
_____
_____
_____
_____

**One thing
I learned this week:**

_____
_____
_____
_____
_____

**I helped someone
this week by:**

_____
_____
_____
_____
_____

**The best thing to
happen this week:**

_____
_____
_____
_____
_____

This week's family blessing:

Our Shabbat this week:
(foods, activities, family, friends, events, pets, etc.)

___

Draw, doodle, stick...

Date _____

This week,
I'm grateful for:
_____
_____
_____
_____
_____

One thing
I learned this week:
_____
_____
_____
_____
_____

I helped someone
this week by:
_____
_____
_____
_____
_____

The best thing to
happen this week:
_____
_____
_____
_____
_____

This week's family blessing:

Our Shabbat this week:
(foods, activities, family, friends, events, pets, etc.)

_____
_____
_____
_____
_____
_____
_____
_____

Draw, doodle, stick...

Date _____

This week,
I'm grateful for:

_____
_____
_____
_____
_____

One thing
I learned this week:

_____
_____
_____
_____
_____

I helped someone
this week by:

_____
_____
_____
_____
_____

The best thing to
happen this week:

_____
_____
_____
_____
_____

This week's family blessing:

Our Shabbat this week:
(foods, activities, family, friends, events, pets, etc.)

_____

_____

_____

_____

_____

_____

_____

_____

Draw, doodle, stick...

Date _____

This week,
I'm grateful for:

_____
_____
_____
_____
_____

One thing
I learned this week:

_____
_____
_____
_____
_____

I helped someone
this week by:

_____
_____
_____
_____
_____

The best thing to
happen this week:

_____
_____
_____
_____
_____

This week's family blessing:

Our Shabbat this week:
(foods, activities, family, friends, events, pets, etc.)

___

Draw, doodle, stick...

Date _____

This week,
I'm grateful for:
_____
_____
_____
_____
_____

One thing
I learned this week:
_____
_____
_____
_____
_____

I helped someone
this week by:
_____
_____
_____
_____
_____

The best thing to
happen this week:
_____
_____
_____
_____
_____

This week's family blessing:

Our Shabbat this week:
(foods, activities, family, friends, events, pets, etc.)

___

Draw, doodle, stick...

Date _____

This week,
I'm grateful for:
_____
_____
_____
_____
_____
_____

One thing
I learned this week:
_____
_____
_____
_____
_____
_____

I helped someone
this week by:
_____
_____
_____
_____
_____
_____

The best thing to
happen this week:
_____
_____
_____
_____
_____
_____

This week's family blessing:

Our Shabbat this week:
(foods, activities, family, friends, events, pets, etc.)

_____
_____
_____
_____
_____
_____
_____
_____

Draw, doodle, stick...

Date _____

This week,
I'm grateful for:
_____
_____
_____
_____
_____

One thing
I learned this week:
_____
_____
_____
_____
_____

I helped someone
this week by:
_____
_____
_____
_____
_____

The best thing to
happen this week:
_____
_____
_____
_____
_____

This week's family blessing:

Our Shabbat this week:
(foods, activities, family, friends, events, pets, etc.)

_____
_____
_____
_____
_____
_____
_____
_____
_____

Draw, doodle, stick...

Date _____

This week,
I'm grateful for:

_____
_____
_____
_____
_____
_____

One thing
I learned this week:

_____
_____
_____
_____
_____
_____

I helped someone
this week by:

_____
_____
_____
_____
_____
_____

The best thing to
happen this week:

_____
_____
_____
_____
_____
_____

This week's family blessing:

Our Shabbat this week:
(foods, activities, family, friends, events, pets, etc.)

_____
_____
_____
_____
_____
_____
_____
_____

Draw, doodle, stick...

Date _____

This week,
I'm grateful for:
_____
_____
_____
_____
_____

One thing
I learned this week:
_____
_____
_____
_____
_____

I helped someone
this week by:
_____
_____
_____
_____
_____

The best thing to
happen this week:
_____
_____
_____
_____
_____

This week's family blessing:

Our Shabbat this week:
(foods, activities, family, friends, events, pets, etc.)

_____
_____
_____
_____
_____
_____
_____
_____
_____

Draw, doodle, stick...

Date _____

This week,
I'm grateful for:

_____
_____
_____
_____
_____

One thing
I learned this week:

_____
_____
_____
_____
_____

I helped someone
this week by:

_____
_____
_____
_____
_____

The best thing to
happen this week:

_____
_____
_____
_____
_____

This week's family blessing:

Our Shabbat this week:
(foods, activities, family, friends, events, pets, etc.)

_____

_____

_____

_____

_____

_____

_____

_____

Draw, doodle, stick...

Date _____

**This week,
I'm grateful for:**

_____
_____
_____
_____
_____
_____

**One thing
I learned this week:**

_____
_____
_____
_____
_____
_____

**I helped someone
this week by:**

_____
_____
_____
_____
_____

**The best thing to
happen this week:**

_____
_____
_____
_____
_____

This week's family blessing:

Our Shabbat this week:
(foods, activities, family, friends, events, pets, etc.)

_____
_____
_____
_____
_____
_____
_____
_____
_____

Draw, doodle, stick...

Date _____

This week,
I'm grateful for:

_____
_____
_____
_____
_____

One thing
I learned this week:

_____
_____
_____
_____
_____

I helped someone
this week by:

_____
_____
_____
_____
_____

The best thing to
happen this week:

_____
_____
_____
_____
_____

This week's family blessing:

Our Shabbat this week:
(foods, activities, family, friends, events, pets, etc.)

_____
_____
_____
_____
_____
_____
_____
_____

Draw, doodle, stick...

Date _____

This week,
I'm grateful for:
_____
_____
_____
_____
_____

One thing
I learned this week:
_____
_____
_____
_____
_____

I helped someone
this week by:
_____
_____
_____
_____
_____

The best thing to
happen this week:
_____
_____
_____
_____
_____

This week's family blessing:

Our Shabbat this week:
(foods, activities, family, friends, events, pets, etc.)

___

Draw, doodle, stick...

Date _____

This week,
I'm grateful for:

_____
_____
_____
_____
_____

One thing
I learned this week:

_____
_____
_____
_____
_____

I helped someone
this week by:

_____
_____
_____
_____
_____

The best thing to
happen this week:

_____
_____
_____
_____
_____

This week's family blessing:

Our Shabbat this week:
(foods, activities, family, friends, events, pets, etc.)

_____
_____
_____
_____
_____
_____
_____
_____
_____

Draw, doodle, stick...

Date _____

This week,
I'm grateful for:

_____
_____
_____
_____
_____

One thing
I learned this week:

_____
_____
_____
_____
_____

I helped someone
this week by:

_____
_____
_____
_____
_____

The best thing to
happen this week:

_____
_____
_____
_____
_____

This week's family blessing:

Our Shabbat this week:
(foods, activities, family, friends, events, pets, etc.)

_____
_____
_____
_____
_____
_____
_____
_____
_____

Draw, doodle, stick...

Date _____

This week,
I'm grateful for:

_____
_____
_____
_____
_____

One thing
I learned this week:

_____
_____
_____
_____
_____

I helped someone
this week by:

_____
_____
_____
_____
_____

The best thing to
happen this week:

_____
_____
_____
_____
_____

This week's family blessing:

Our Shabbat this week:
(foods, activities, family, friends, events, pets, etc.)

_____
_____
_____
_____
_____
_____
_____
_____

Draw, doodle, stick...

Date _____

This week,
I'm grateful for:

_____
_____
_____
_____
_____
_____

One thing
I learned this week:

_____
_____
_____
_____
_____
_____

I helped someone
this week by:

_____
_____
_____
_____
_____
_____

The best thing to
happen this week:

_____
_____
_____
_____
_____
_____

This week's family blessing:

Our Shabbat this week:
(foods, activities, family, friends, events, pets, etc.)

_____
_____
_____
_____
_____
_____
_____
_____
_____

Draw, doodle, stick…

Date _____

This week,
I'm grateful for:

_____
_____
_____
_____
_____

One thing
I learned this week:

_____
_____
_____
_____
_____

I helped someone
this week by:

_____
_____
_____
_____
_____

The best thing to
happen this week:

_____
_____
_____
_____
_____

This week's family blessing:

Our Shabbat this week:
(foods, activities, family, friends, events, pets, etc.)

_____
_____
_____
_____
_____
_____
_____
_____
_____

Draw, doodle, stick...

Date _____

**This week,
I'm grateful for:**
_____
_____
_____
_____
_____
_____

**One thing
I learned this week:**
_____
_____
_____
_____
_____
_____

**I helped someone
this week by:**
_____
_____
_____
_____
_____
_____

**The best thing to
happen this week:**
_____
_____
_____
_____
_____
_____

This week's family blessing:

Our Shabbat this week:
(foods, activities, family, friends, events, pets, etc.)

_____
_____
_____
_____
_____
_____
_____
_____

Draw, doodle, stick...

Date _____

This week,
I'm grateful for:

_____
_____
_____
_____
_____

One thing
I learned this week:

_____
_____
_____
_____
_____

I helped someone
this week by:

_____
_____
_____
_____
_____

The best thing to
happen this week:

_____
_____
_____
_____
_____

This week's family blessing:

Our Shabbat this week:
(foods, activities, family, friends, events, pets, etc.)

_____
_____
_____
_____
_____
_____
_____
_____
_____

Draw, doodle, stick...

Date _____

This week,
I'm grateful for:

_____
_____
_____
_____
_____

One thing
I learned this week:

_____
_____
_____
_____
_____

I helped someone
this week by:

_____
_____
_____
_____
_____

The best thing to
happen this week:

_____
_____
_____
_____
_____

This week's family blessing:

Our Shabbat this week:
(foods, activities, family, friends, events, pets, etc.)

Draw, doodle, stick...

Date _____

This week,
I'm grateful for:
_____
_____
_____
_____
_____

One thing
I learned this week:
_____
_____
_____
_____
_____

I helped someone
this week by:
_____
_____
_____
_____
_____

The best thing to
happen this week:
_____
_____
_____
_____
_____

This week's family blessing:

Our Shabbat this week:
(foods, activities, family, friends, events, pets, etc.)

_____
_____
_____
_____
_____
_____
_____
_____

Draw, doodle, stick...

Date _____

This week,
I'm grateful for:

_____
_____
_____
_____
_____

One thing
I learned this week:

_____
_____
_____
_____
_____

I helped someone
this week by:

_____
_____
_____
_____
_____

The best thing to
happen this week:

_____
_____
_____
_____
_____

This week's family blessing:

Our Shabbat this week:
(foods, activities, family, friends, events, pets, etc.)

_____
_____
_____
_____
_____
_____
_____
_____
_____

Draw, doodle, stick...

Date _____

This week,
I'm grateful for:

_____
_____
_____
_____
_____

One thing
I learned this week:

_____
_____
_____
_____
_____

I helped someone
this week by:

_____
_____
_____
_____

The best thing to
happen this week:

_____
_____
_____
_____

This week's family blessing:

Our Shabbat this week:
(foods, activities, family, friends, events, pets, etc.)

_____
_____
_____
_____
_____
_____
_____
_____
_____

Draw, doodle, stick...

Date _____

This week,
I'm grateful for:

_____
_____
_____
_____
_____

One thing
I learned this week:

_____
_____
_____
_____
_____

I helped someone
this week by:

_____
_____
_____
_____
_____

The best thing to
happen this week:

_____
_____
_____
_____
_____

This week's family blessing:

Our Shabbat this week:
(foods, activities, family, friends, events, pets, etc.)

_____
_____
_____
_____
_____
_____
_____
_____

Draw, doodle, stick...

Date _____

This week,
I'm grateful for:
_____
_____
_____
_____
_____

One thing
I learned this week:
_____
_____
_____
_____
_____

I helped someone
this week by:
_____
_____
_____
_____
_____

The best thing to
happen this week:
_____
_____
_____
_____
_____

This week's family blessing:

Our Shabbat this week:
(foods, activities, family, friends, events, pets, etc.)

_____
_____
_____
_____
_____
_____
_____
_____

Draw, doodle, stick...

Date _____

This week,
I'm grateful for:
_____
_____
_____
_____
_____

One thing
I learned this week:
_____
_____
_____
_____
_____

I helped someone
this week by:
_____
_____
_____
_____
_____

The best thing to
happen this week:
_____
_____
_____
_____
_____

This week's family blessing:

Our Shabbat this week:
(foods, activities, family, friends, events, pets, etc.)

_____
_____
_____
_____
_____
_____
_____
_____
_____

Draw, doodle, stick...

Date _____

**This week,
I'm grateful for:**
_____
_____
_____
_____
_____

**One thing
I learned this week:**
_____
_____
_____
_____
_____

**I helped someone
this week by:**
_____
_____
_____
_____
_____

**The best thing to
happen this week:**
_____
_____
_____
_____
_____

This week's family blessing:

Our Shabbat this week:
(foods, activities, family, friends, events, pets, etc.)

_____
_____
_____
_____
_____
_____
_____
_____
_____

Draw, doodle, stick...

Date _____

**This week,
I'm grateful for:**

_____
_____
_____
_____
_____

**One thing
I learned this week:**

_____
_____
_____
_____
_____

**I helped someone
this week by:**

_____
_____
_____
_____
_____

**The best thing to
happen this week:**

_____
_____
_____
_____
_____

This week's family blessing:

Our Shabbat this week:
(foods, activities, family, friends, events, pets, etc.)

Draw, doodle, stick...

Date _____

**This week,
I'm grateful for:**

_____
_____
_____
_____
_____

**One thing
I learned this week:**

_____
_____
_____
_____
_____

**I helped someone
this week by:**

_____
_____
_____
_____
_____

**The best thing to
happen this week:**

_____
_____
_____
_____
_____

This week's family blessing:

Our Shabbat this week:
(foods, activities, family, friends, events, pets, etc.)

_____
_____
_____
_____
_____
_____
_____
_____
_____

Draw, doodle, stick...

Date _____

This week,
I'm grateful for:
_____
_____
_____
_____
_____

One thing
I learned this week:
_____
_____
_____
_____
_____

I helped someone
this week by:
_____
_____
_____
_____
_____

The best thing to
happen this week:
_____
_____
_____
_____
_____

This week's family blessing:

Our Shabbat this week:
(foods, activities, family, friends, events, pets, etc.)

_____
_____
_____
_____
_____
_____
_____
_____

Draw, doodle, stick...

Date _____

This week,
I'm grateful for:

_____
_____
_____
_____
_____

One thing
I learned this week:

_____
_____
_____
_____
_____

I helped someone
this week by:

_____
_____
_____
_____
_____

The best thing to
happen this week:

_____
_____
_____
_____
_____

This week's family blessing:

Our Shabbat this week:
(foods, activities, family, friends, events, pets, etc.)

_____
_____
_____
_____
_____
_____
_____
_____
_____

Draw, doodle, stick...

Date _____

This week,
I'm grateful for:
_____
_____
_____
_____
_____

One thing
I learned this week:
_____
_____
_____
_____
_____

I helped someone
this week by:
_____
_____
_____
_____
_____

The best thing to
happen this week:
_____
_____
_____
_____
_____

This week's family blessing:

Our Shabbat this week:
(foods, activities, family, friends, events, pets, etc.)

_____
_____
_____
_____
_____
_____
_____
_____
_____

Draw, doodle, stick…

Date _____

**This week,
I'm grateful for:**

_____
_____
_____
_____
_____

**One thing
I learned this week:**

_____
_____
_____
_____
_____

**I helped someone
this week by:**

_____
_____
_____
_____
_____

**The best thing to
happen this week:**

_____
_____
_____
_____
_____

This week's family blessing:

Our Shabbat this week:
(foods, activities, family, friends, events, pets, etc.)

___

Draw, doodle, stick...

Date _____

This week,
I'm grateful for:
_____
_____
_____
_____
_____

One thing
I learned this week:
_____
_____
_____
_____
_____

I helped someone
this week by:
_____
_____
_____
_____
_____

The best thing to
happen this week:
_____
_____
_____
_____
_____

This week's family blessing:

Our Shabbat this week:
(foods, activities, family, friends, events, pets, etc.)

___

Draw, doodle, stick...

Date _____

**This week,
I'm grateful for:**
_____
_____
_____
_____
_____

**One thing
I learned this week:**
_____
_____
_____
_____
_____

**I helped someone
this week by:**
_____
_____
_____
_____
_____

**The best thing to
happen this week:**
_____
_____
_____
_____
_____

This week's family blessing:

Our Shabbat this week:
(foods, activities, family, friends, events, pets, etc.)

Draw, doodle, stick...

Date _____

This week,
I'm grateful for:
_____
_____
_____
_____
_____

One thing
I learned this week:
_____
_____
_____
_____
_____

I helped someone
this week by:
_____
_____
_____
_____
_____

The best thing to
happen this week:
_____
_____
_____
_____
_____

This week's family blessing:

Our Shabbat this week:
(foods, activities, family, friends, events, pets, etc.)

___

Draw, doodle, stick...

Date _____

This week,
I'm grateful for:
_____
_____
_____
_____
_____

One thing
I learned this week:
_____
_____
_____
_____
_____

I helped someone
this week by:
_____
_____
_____
_____
_____

The best thing to
happen this week:
_____
_____
_____
_____
_____

This week's family blessing:

Our Shabbat this week:
(foods, activities, family, friends, events, pets, etc.)

_____
_____
_____
_____
_____
_____
_____
_____
_____

Draw, doodle, stick...

Date _____

This week,
I'm grateful for:
_____
_____
_____
_____
_____

One thing
I learned this week:
_____
_____
_____
_____
_____

I helped someone
this week by:
_____
_____
_____
_____
_____

The best thing to
happen this week:
_____
_____
_____
_____
_____

This week's family blessing:

Our Shabbat this week:
(foods, activities, family, friends, events, pets, etc.)

_____
_____
_____
_____
_____
_____
_____
_____

Draw, doodle, stick...

Date _____

**This week,
I'm grateful for:**

_____
_____
_____
_____
_____

**One thing
I learned this week:**

_____
_____
_____
_____
_____

**I helped someone
this week by:**

_____
_____
_____
_____
_____

**The best thing to
happen this week:**

_____
_____
_____
_____
_____

This week's family blessing:

Our Shabbat this week:
(foods, activities, family, friends, events, pets, etc.)

_____
_____
_____
_____
_____
_____
_____
_____

Draw, doodle, stick...

Date _____

This week,
I'm grateful for:
_____
_____
_____
_____
_____

One thing
I learned this week:
_____
_____
_____
_____
_____

I helped someone
this week by:
_____
_____
_____
_____
_____

The best thing to
happen this week:
_____
_____
_____
_____
_____

This week's family blessing:

Our Shabbat this week:
(foods, activities, family, friends, events, pets, etc.)

_____
_____
_____
_____
_____
_____
_____
_____

Draw, doodle, stick...

Date _____

This week,
I'm grateful for:

_____
_____
_____
_____
_____

One thing
I learned this week:

_____
_____
_____
_____
_____

I helped someone
this week by:

_____
_____
_____
_____
_____

The best thing to
happen this week:

_____
_____
_____
_____
_____

This week's family blessing:

Our Shabbat this week:
(foods, activities, family, friends, events, pets, etc.)

_____
_____
_____
_____
_____
_____
_____
_____
_____

Draw, doodle, stick...

Date _____

This week,
I'm grateful for:
_____
_____
_____
_____
_____

One thing
I learned this week:
_____
_____
_____
_____
_____

I helped someone
this week by:
_____
_____
_____
_____
_____

The best thing to
happen this week:
_____
_____
_____
_____
_____

This week's family blessing:

Our Shabbat this week:
(foods, activities, family, friends, events, pets, etc.)

_____
_____
_____
_____
_____
_____
_____
_____

Draw, doodle, stick...

Date _____

This week, I'm grateful for:

_____
_____
_____
_____
_____

One thing I learned this week:

_____
_____
_____
_____
_____

I helped someone this week by:

_____
_____
_____
_____
_____

The best thing to happen this week:

_____
_____
_____
_____
_____

This week's family blessing:

Our Shabbat this week:
(foods, activities, family, friends, events, pets, etc.)

Draw, doodle, stick...

Date _____

This week,
I'm grateful for:

_____
_____
_____
_____
_____

One thing
I learned this week:

_____
_____
_____
_____
_____

I helped someone
this week by:

_____
_____
_____
_____
_____

The best thing to
happen this week:

_____
_____
_____
_____
_____

This week's family blessing:

Our Shabbat this week:
(foods, activities, family, friends, events, pets, etc.)

Draw, doodle, stick...

Date _____

This week,
I'm grateful for:

_____
_____
_____
_____
_____

One thing
I learned this week:

_____
_____
_____
_____
_____

I helped someone
this week by:

_____
_____
_____
_____
_____

The best thing to
happen this week:

_____
_____
_____
_____
_____

This week's family blessing:

Our Shabbat this week:
(foods, activities, family, friends, events, pets, etc.)

_____
_____
_____
_____
_____
_____
_____
_____

Draw, doodle, stick...

www.ingramcontent.com/pod-product-compliance
Lightning Source LLC
Chambersburg PA
CBHW060457300426
44113CB00016B/2619